Free From Guilt And Condemnation

Free From Guilt And Condemnation

by

Don Hughes

HARRISON HOUSE
Tulsa, Oklahoma

Unless otherwise indicated,
all Scripture quotations are taken from
the *King James Version* of the Bible.

10 Printing

Free From Guilt And Condemnation
ISBN 0-89274-048-5
Copyright © 1977 by Don Hughes
P. O. Box 840
Broken Arrow, Oklahoma 74013

Published by Harrison House, Inc.
P. O. Box 35035
Tulsa, Oklahoma 74153

Printed in the United States of America.
All rights reserved under International Copyright Law.
Contents and/or cover may not be reproduced in whole or
in part in any form without the express written consent
of the Publisher.

FREE FROM GUILT AND CONDEMNATION

For we know that the law is spiritual: but I am carnal, sold under sin. For that which I do I allow not: for what I would, that do I not; but what I hate, that do I. If then I do that which I would not, I consent unto the law that it is good.

Now then it is no more I that do it, but sin that dwelleth in me. For I know that in me (that is, in my flesh,) dwelleth no good thing: for to will is present with me; but how to perform that which is good I find not. For the good that I would I do not: but the evil which I would not, that I do.

Now if I do that I would not, it is no more I that do it, but sin that dwelleth in me. I find then a law, that, when I would do good, evil is present with me. For I delight in the law of God after the inward man: But I see another law in my members, warring against the law of my mind, and bringing me into captivity to the law of sin which is in my members.

O wretched man that I am! who shall deliver me from the body of this death? I thank God through Jesus Christ our Lord.

So then with the mind I myself serve the law of God; but with the flesh the law of sin. ***There is therefore now no condemnation to them which are in Christ Jesus,*** *who walk not after the flesh, but after the Spirit* (Romans 7:14-8:1).

Many people have fallen short of the glory of God, especially in some realm of service, or when some sin seems to be prevalent in their lives. Finding no way to conquer it, they live under constant guilt and condemnation. The Bible teaches us that when God forgives our sins, He removes them as far as the east is from the west, and He remembers them no more. God **forgives** you of your sins. He does not just **cover** them. He **removes** them. The Old Testament sacrifices could only **cover**, but the blood of Christ **removes.**

If He forgives, removes and forgets your sins, your obligation is also to forget them. If God forgives you, you forgive yourself. "Happy is the man that condemneth not himself" (Romans 14:22). Have any of you ever had past sins brought up to you by the devil? I mean sins that have been under the blood for years. He tries to make you think that you're not worthy to receive God's blessings. He will get you feeling sorry for yourself. You have to get this self-pity attitude out of your heart.

Many times our approach to God has been wrong when we say, "Lord, I'm not worthy." I remember one time while praying and feeling sorry for myself, I was murmuring to God — complaining — trying to get God to feel sorry for me. I kept telling God how unworthy I was. Suddenly, He spoke to my inner man, "You are too worthy!" "I am?" "Yes, you sure are. Don't you believe My Bible?" He had me on the spot, because I had always said I did. "Yes, Lord, I believe it." He said, "How about Ephesians 2:10?" So I turned there and read, "Ye are the workmanship of God created in Christ Jesus unto good works."

All of a sudden it became real to me. I remembered in the Bible when God created something, He looked at it and said, "It is good." He never made anything that was bad. He didn't create anything that was worthless or unworthy. He knows how to build it good.

When He recreated you and me, He did a good job.

What we need to do is to begin seeing ourselves as God sees us. I'm glad that God doesn't see me like I see myself. When He looks at me, He sees Christ. He sees the finished product. So let's begin to look at ourselves as God sees us. When we do this, we are going to be better able to live without guilt and condemnation. Hosea said, "My people are destroyed for a lack of knowledge" (Hosea 4:6).

If we don't understand the full provision that Christ provided for us through His death on the cross, if we don't understand what our inheritance involves, if we don't know how to pray for and receive what rightly belongs to us, we're going to be destroyed. Solomon said, "through knowledge shall the just be delivered" (Proverbs 11:9). Isaiah 5:13 reads, "Therefore my people are gone into captivity because they have no knowledge." If you have no knowledge, you are going to put yourself into captivity.

You must understand that guilt and condemnation does not have to reign over you.

The devil will try to take advantage of your ignorance and keep you in bondage. However, the Lord said, "You shall KNOW the truth, and the truth shall set you free" (John 8:32).

There is a place we can come to in Christ where there is no condemnation, and it is arrived at through knowledge. Through the first seven chapters of Romans, the Holy Spirit is only referred to one time. But, by the time you get into chapter eight, which is often referred to as the victory chapter, Paul mentions the Holy Spirit nineteen times.

It is important what you do with the Holy Spirit and what the Holy Spirit does in you. Your flesh and your spirit lust against each other. The human spirit wants to fellowship with God. Your spirit is the real you. When you go to a funeral, you look at a loved one or a friend, and you say, "They're not really there." What do you mean? You are looking at them. You mean that their spirit (the part that wants to fellowship with God) is not there. The body is only an earthly house (2 Cor. 5:1).

Paul says, "If we walk in the Spirit, we shall not fulfill the lust of the flesh"

(Galatians 5:16). We need to know what it means to walk in the Spirit. It's more than just a term in the Bible. Find out how to walk in the Spirit. Just because you are baptized in the Holy Spirit does not necessarily mean that you are walking in the Spirit. The baptism is a step in the right direction, but it does not guarantee that you will continue to walk in the Spirit. It does not guarantee that you will permit the Spirit of God to dictate to your heart. If you walk in the Spirit, you will not fulfill the lust of the flesh.

I think we need a more clear understanding of the finished work of Jesus. I challenge you to notice when Paul writes in the past tense. The Amplified translation is good for putting statements in the proper tenses. Whenever the past tense is used, especially in regard to things that Christ has bought for us, notice it — that means it is already ours.

We need to learn how to walk in the light of the finished work of God. Most of us are going about **trying** to be like Christ. We're going about **trying** to keep the law. And we put ourselves right back under the bondage of legalism. Nobody can keep the law. The Old Testament people proved that. Jesus met the full requirements of the law; He fulfilled righteousness for us and imputed it unto us (2 Cor. 5:21). We need to live in the completed work of the cross.

In Colossians chapter two, we have a picture of the finished work of Christ. Most of us are, within ourselves, trying to do these things. Romans 10:3 reads, *For they being ignorant of God's righteousness, and going about to establish their own righteousness, have not submitted themselves unto the righteousness of God.* We are not to go around **trying** to be righteous, we are to **submit** ourselves to the righteousness of God. When we do this, we are "righteous." We cannot attain righteousness ourselves. Christ is the end of the law for them that believed. He was the only one that met the requirements. When we put ourselves "in Him," we are righteous.

"For in Him dwelleth all the fulness of the Godhead bodily" (Colossians 2:9). As we read through these verses, I want you to notice the things that are already finished for us. **"And you are complete in him"** (v. 10). The Amplified translation says, **"You are made full."** When this truth sinks into your heart, you won't have to approach God anymore and say, "Lord, fill my cup." There is really nothing else He can do. The whole thing is a provision in our inheritance. It's not a matter of you trying to get yourself filled, but rather a matter of walking in the fullness of what has already been provided. There is nothing else God has to do.

*Ye are complete in Him which is the head of all principality and power: In whom also **ye are circumcised** with the circumcision made without hands, in putting off the body of the sins of the flesh by the circumcision of Christ* (v. 10-11).

In the circumcision of Christ, we are circumcised in heart. Yet I find many people **trying** to circumcise the heart, **trying** to be righteous, **trying** to live above sin; and the harder they try, the more guilt and condemnation they undergo when they fail. It's not a matter of **trying**; it's a matter of **resting.** Jesus said, "It is finished." **Rest in it.** The **knowledge** of this truth will set you free.

"**Buried with him in baptism** (a finished work), wherein also ye **are risen** with Him . . ." (v. 12). Notice two things — **you are**

buried with Him, and **you are risen** with Him. If you are risen with Him, where are you? Where is He? IN HEAVENLY PLACES! Where are these heavenly places? "Far above all principalities and powers" (Eph. 1:21). You are sitting in the heavenlies with God (Eph. 2:6). If you are up there with Him, then that puts all the principalities and powers under your feet, doesn't it? But, you've got to **know it AND act upon it.**

That's part of your inheritance. See yourself as God sees you. Put yourself where God puts you. God sees the finished product. We were chosen in Christ before the foundation of the world.

That thrills my heart every time I think about it. If I tend to get a little discouraged, I begin to think about some of these tremendous truths in the Word of God. Just think, before the foundation of the world, way back in eternity past, God chose me to have a part in this last-day revival; and here I am **trying** instead of **resting** in something He completed before the foundation of the world. All I have to do is rest in what He has planned. When I fit into His plan, and flow with His Spirit, I am going to end up at my, or rather, His destination.

*And you, **being dead** in your sins and the uncircumcision of your flesh, **hath he quickened** together with him, **having forgiven** all trespasses, **blotting out** the handwriting of ordinances that was against us, which was contrary to us, and **took** it out of the way, nailing it to His cross* . . . (vv. 13-14). Notice the things that are already yours. The law brought a knowledge of sin. The law made you realize you were a sinner — not the obedience to it, but the guilt of it.

"And having spoiled principalities and powers, He made a shew of them openly, triumphing over them in it" (v. 15). (The "it" refers to the "cross" of v. 14). Jesus has already defeated the devil. The study of numerology in Scripture is interesting. Like anything else, you can go overboard on it and get off into error. But, by the same token, every word of God, every jot and tittle, is inspired by God. Numbers mean something.

For example, "six" is the number of man. "Six-six-six" is the amplification of man to show that even the anti-christ, who goes by that number, really falls short of the glory of God, even though he says he is God. The number "seven" means completeness and represents God and His completed work.

The number "eight," for example, goes a little beyond being complete; it represents resurrection life. You don't have to wait until you are resurrected to live a resurrected (overcoming) life. The reason I say this is because all the provision for the resurrected life is already made in Christ. If you are in Christ and recognize this truth, then you will not have to live under guilt and condemnation. You can begin to rise and walk in a newness of life. "Ye are of God, little children, and **have overcome them . . .**" (1 John 4:4).

Between verses nine and fifteen of Colossians two can be found eight truths that are already ours. "Eight" — the resurrected life. If we have a knowledge of the finished work of Jesus Christ, we can live free of guilt and condemnation.

What shall we say then? Shall we continue in sin, that grace may abound? God forbid.

> *How shall we, that are dead to sin, live any longer therein? Know ye not, that so many of us as were baptized into Jesus Christ were baptized into His death?*
>
> *Therefore we are buried with Him by baptism into death: that like as Christ was raised up from the dead by the glory of the Father, even so we also should walk in newness of life.*
>
> *For if we have been planted together in the likeness of His death, we shall be also in the likeness of His resurrection:*
>
> ***Knowing this,*** *that our old man is crucified with Him, that the body of sin might be destroyed, that henceforth we should not serve sin* (Romans 6:1-6).

For so long a time, I kept trying to crucify my flesh. There is a sense in which **we** are to do something. Paul said, "Mortify the deeds of the flesh." However, we need to learn how to turn our will over to God and let Him do it for us. I would read where Paul said, "I am crucified with Christ. Nevertheless, I live, yet not I, but Christ liveth in me" (Gal. 2:20). I would reply, "Oh, Lord, if I could just crucify my flesh, I'd be like Paul." I was able to win over a few. A strong "self-willed" person can conquer some problems.

There were many areas where I could not. The more I tried, the more I realized it was impossible. I started feeling guilty and condemned. I kept thinking, somehow in the life of Paul, he got to the point where he was able to crucify his flesh. Then the truth of "resting in the finished work" began to open to me.

When you stop to think about it, what do you do when you crucify yourself? You have to build yourself a cross, because Jesus was crucified on the cross. So you build yourself a cross and lay it down. Then you lay yourself on the cross — you're going to crucify the flesh. You get a bucket of nails and a hammer. You take a nail and the hammer and you reach down and drive a nail through your two feet. That much is done. You lay your left arm out and drive a spike through your hand. Then, what do you do with your other hand? How are you going to get it crucified? When I began to see this, the Lord said to me that the most I could do for myself was a half job. I said, "Lord, that's right." We are destroyed for a lack of knowledge. Paul used two terms in his writings. "Don't be ignorant of this." Then when he wanted to be a little more polite, he said, "Knowing this . . . ." If you don't know it, you're ignorant of it.

Notice what he said in Romans 6:6: "Knowing this," and in verse three, "Know ye not?" Or, "Don't you know that it is already done?" When I saw this, a new truth opened to me. "Knowing this, that our old man IS crucified."

I said, "Lord, how does that work? I see it, I believe it, it's there, but I don't understand it." Then He gave me an illustration. Do you remember how Abraham, coming back from a war, stopped to see the King of Salem and paid tithes to Melchizedek? And yet the Bible says that Levi, of the tribe of Levi, of the priesthood of God, paid tithes to Melchizedek through Abraham, and yet he wasn't born until four hundred years later.

He was in the loins of Abraham. In the mind of God it was already done. Levi paid tithes through Abraham to Melchizedek, King of Salem and type of Christ, maybe even the pre-incarnate Christ. All of a sudden, I began to see something. What did Paul mean in

Ephesians 1:5 when he said that we were chosen in Christ before the foundation of the world? God knew who would respond to the Gospel call. He knew before the foundation of the world who would say *yes* to Christ and who sould say *no*. **Through his knowledge He chose.**

Two thousand years ago, when Christ hung on the cross, we, who were chosen in Him before the foundation of the world, also hung there with Him. Because He died for the sins of Don Hughes, my sins were nailed to that cross with him. He blotted them out. He met the requirements of the law. The requirements of the law for sin is death. God said, "You, Don Hughes, have died. You have been crucified. I nailed you to the cross with Jesus two thousand years ago." It is a finished work. Paul said, **"Know this."**

If you don't know it, you are going to keep trying to do it yourself. When I realized that it was a finished work, that I didn't have to constantly battle sin, that I could permit the Holy Spirit to lead me, that I could walk in the Spirit, and not fulfill the lust of the flesh, victory became mine.

"Knowing this, the old man is crucified with Him that the body of sin might be destroyed, that henceforth we should not **serve** sin. For he that is dead is **freed** from sin" (v. 7). Paul declared that we have already died in Christ. If we have already died in Christ, we are free. We are free from what? From serving sin. We are free from the guilt and condemnation of it. We don't have to live under that bondage.

Now if we be dead with Christ, we believe that we shall also live with him: KNOWING that Christ being raised from the dead dieth no more; death hath no more dominion over him (v. 8-9). I'll tell you why I think we still live under guilt and condemnation for our failures, because we don't understand verse eleven, or at least we haven't applied it to ourselves. Notice what this whole passage says: Christ died, He was freed, we are in Him, we are crucified, we are freed, we are dead. "Likewise, reckon yourselves dead indeed into sin" (v.11). Otherwise, picture yourself that way. Look at yourself with your shortcomings and your problems, but look at yourself as God sees you. Don't get a picture of yourself as an unworthy, down and out, defeated person.

If that's the picture you have of yourself, you'll never rise to victory. I meet people like this every day. My heart goes out to them. You can talk to them, and talk to them, but they don't understand what you are saying. Paul goes on to say: "Let not sin therefore reign in your mortal body, that ye should obey it in the lusts thereof. Neither yield ye your members as instruments of unrighteousness unto sin: but yield yourselves unto God, as those that are alive from the dead, and your members as instruments of righteousness unto God. For sin shall not have dominion over you . . ." (v. 12-14). Praise God for this truth!

Sin shall not lord it over you, provided you **know this,** and provided you **reckon yourself dead** unto sin. Sin will not lord it over you. Sin will not dominate you, for you are not under the law. If you were under the law, it would lord it over you. But you are not under the law, you are under Christ. He was the end of the law of righteousness for all those who believe. *Know ye not, that to whom ye yield yourselves servants to obey, his servants ye are to whom you obey; whether of sin unto death, or of obedience unto righteousness?* (v. 16).

This does not mean that you do not have to obey God's laws.

Let me caution you here. In Romans 6:1 Paul felt he had to insert this lest he be misunderstood. "What shall we say then? Shall we continue in sin, that grace may abound? God forbid." We are not giving you a license to sin, but we are telling you that sin doesn't have to lord it over you. Sin doesn't have to defeat and conquer you. You don't have to yield to sin. "Obedience unto righteousness." *Wherefore, my brethren, ye also are become dead to the law by the body of Christ; that ye should be married to another* (Romans 7:4). *Now we are delivered from the law* (Romans 7:6).

I had a man come to me once who was very troubled and perplexed, because on his job he felt that he was a failure in being a witness for Jesus Christ. The devil played upon this in his life. This man was living under guilt and condemnation. Then I showed him that even Paul had that kind of battle, even Paul said, "the things I don't want to do, those are the things I end up doing. I'm a wretched man." How many of you know that if you're living under guilt and condemnation, you are a wretched man? You're miserable. Paul continued to say, "Who shall deliver me from this?" He gave the answer, "I thank God through Jesus Christ." Because through Jesus Christ we were nailed to the cross with Him.

Most of our battles go on in our minds. Second Corinthians 4:4 tells us that the god of this world (Satan) blinds the minds of those who believe not. We can eliminate the battle of our minds through knowledge. We can rise above it. *Renew the mind* (Romans 12:2). *And these things write we unto you, that your joy may be full* (1 John 1:4). If you are living under guilt and condemnation, your joy cannot be full.

Whosoever abideth in Him sinneth not: whosoever sinneth hath not seen Him, neither known Him. Little children, let no man deceive you: he that doeth righteousness is righteous, even as He is righteous. He that committeth sin is of the devil; for the devil sinneth from the beginning.

For this purpose the Son of God was manifested, that He might destroy the works of the devil. Whosoever is born of God doth not commit sin; for His seed remaineth in him: and he cannot sin, because he is born of God (1 John 3:6-9).

This is a rather confusing verse at first glance, until you get into the tenses used in the Greek. If you read some other translations, I think it will clarify the passage. The Amplified translation certainly will. Marginal renderings will also do it. It reads like this, "Whosoever abideth in Him does not **continually practice sinning:** whosoever **continually practices sinning** has not seen Him." This doesn't mean that you might not have a problem in your life. John said: *My little children, these things write I unto you, that ye sin not. And if any man sin, we have an advocate with the Father, Jesus Christ the righteous* (1 John 2:1). If we fail God, we are to "confess our sins" (1 John 1:9). When we do, God forgives and forgets.

"He that continually practices sin is of the devil, but the Son of God was manifested that He might destroy the works of the devil. Whosoever is born of God does not continually practice sinning, for his seed remaineth in him and he cannot continually practice sinning." You don't have a license to sin because you are freed from the guilt of it.

This then is the message which we have heard of Him, and declare unto you, that God is light, and in Him is no darkness at all. If we say that we have fellowship with him, and walk in darkness, we lie . . . (1 John 1:5-6). It is very easy to go around saying, "I'm in Christ." But the Bible says, "Ye shall know them by their fruits." There are many people saying, "I'm in Christ," and they are not bearing any fruit.

But if we walk in the light, as He is in the light, we have fellowship one with another, and the blood of Jesus Christ His Son cleanseth us from all sin (v. 7). In the Greek, this is also in the "continuing" tense. This is what he is really saying: "The blood of Jesus Christ His Son continually cleanses."

In the Old Testament, the blood of lambs couldn't do that. Every time the people did something wrong, they had to bring a sacrifice. Once a year, the priest went through his ceremonial rites. He entered into the Holy of Holies, offering a sacrifice for himself and for the sins of the people. He had to do that year after year, because that offering could only COVER. But when Christ died, His blood was put into a perpetual motion of cleansing. When we come to Christ and are saved, He REMOVES all of our past sins. He said, "I remember them no more." When we are saved, sin no longer lords it over us. The power of sin has been broken.

If any man sin, if he slips or fails, he has an advocate in Jesus Christ, the Righteous (1 John 2:1), because His blood is in continual motion. So what do we do? We apply verse nine where it reads: "If we confess our sins . . ." This is what we must do. Otherwise, you are going to be yielding yourselves as instruments of unrighteousness, and to whom you yield yourselves servants to obey, his servants you are (Romans 6:16). Aren't you glad that God made provision that if you happen to slip, you can still keep an unbroken fellowship with Him? *If we confess our sins, He is faithful and just to forgive us our sins, and to cleanse us from all unrighteousness* (1 John 1:9).

Our obligation, if we commit a sin, is to confess it to God. The blood of Jesus Christ, in a perpetual motion, cleanses us of that sin. He does the same thing with that sin as He did with all the sins before we got saved. He blots it out. He erases it from our account. He removes it as far as the east is from the west. He doesn't remember it any more.

If He doesn't remember it any more, you forget it, too. Don't feel so guilty having failed. Pick yourself up by the bootstraps, and say, "God, I'm sorry. I missed it. Forgive me," and keep pressing toward the mark. This is what Paul did.

I'll show you where some of us fail. Let's say it is 7:00 o'clock in the morning (it is so easy to miss God that early). You get up grouchy, hard to live with. In that frame of mind you get mad, have an argument, leave the house mad and hurt. You have committed a sin. If you are like most people, you will let that go all day, and at night time, just before you go to bed, what do you do? You say, "Lord, forgive me of all my sins." We say that word "all" because we don't want to name the sins.

David said, "If I regard iniquity in my heart, God will not hear me." So what happens at 3:00 o'clock in the afternoon? An emergency arises. You try to pray, but the answer doesn't come. When you commit sin, confess it right then. Keep your fellowship with God going. Keep the perpetual blood of Christ working; so that when you have to call on God, He will hear. He's faithful and just to forgive you, and to cleanse you from all unrighteousness. Don't walk under guilt and condemnation. In John 3:19, we read, "And **this is the condemnation**, that light is come into the world . . ." Why? Because light condemns the world of darkness. **That's the condemnation.** We are walking in the light because we are confessing our sins, because we are keeping an unbroken fellowship with God, thus we are not under condemnation.

If we say that we have no sin (meaning a sin nature), *we deceive ourselves, and the truth is not in us . . . If we say that we have not sinned* (committed the sin act), *we make Him a liar, and His word is not in us* (1 John 1:8, 10). The Word says, *"All* have sinned and come short of the glory of God." But, "If we confess our sins, He is faithful and just to forgive us, and to cleanse us from all unrighteousness."

We are exhorted in 1 Timothy 3:6 not to put a novice in office: "Not a novice lest being lifted up with pride he fall into condemnation." You see, this is a growing process.

We have to learn certain truths. We have to know our rights and privileges in the Lord. When we learn these truths, we can begin to rise above the guilt and condemnation.

I'm not saying that we ought to go around failing God; but if you do, recognize that you can confess it, go on with God, and not live under guilt and failure. Why? Because Christ is the end of the law. Get yourself out from under the bondage of the law and the legalistic approach of the law. Get under grace, get under the love of God, rest in the Holy Spirit, and you will not fulfill the lust of the flesh.

Many are kept in bondage for going to doctors or taking medicines once they started to stand on faith. Don't let the devil trick you that way. Maturing is a continual process. Keep your faith growing. Don't let failing defeat you. Say, "I may have lost that battle, devil, but I am not going to lose the war. I resist you in the Name of Jesus." Stay in the "good fight of faith." Confess your failings. Accept your forgiveness and press on with God. Hold fast your confession of faith without wavering (Heb. 10:23). It is through faith and patience that we inherit the promises (Heb. 6:12, 15).

Paul's exhortation to us was: *Forgetting those things which are behind, and reaching forth unto those things which are before, I press toward the mark for the prize of the high calling of God in Christ Jesus* (Phil. 3:13-14).

There is therefore now no condemnation to them which are in Christ Jesus (Romans 8:1).

To receive Don Hughes' publication,
The Reigning Life, you may write:

Don Hughes Evangelistic Assn.
P. O. Box Box 840
Broken Arrow, OK 74013

*Feel free to include your prayer requests
and comments when you write.*

Don Hughes, an anointed Bible teacher, has been in the ministry since 1958. In 1962, while attending Bible school to become a Baptist minister, he received the Baptism of the Holy Spirit.

Don has been traveling around the world since 1971, teaching pastors and their churches how to reign in life by believing the uncompromised Word of God. Don teaches with simplicity, preparing the Body of Christ for Christ's soon return. His literature has reached into over 70 countries.

A frequent guest of the P.T.L. Club and at Full Gospel Businessmen International conventions, Don has also taught at Christ For The Nations Bible Institute and spoken at Kenneth Hagin's Campmeeting.

Available from Harrison House Books by Don Hughes

Paul's Thorn

Free From Guilt and Condemnation

HARRISON HOUSE
P. O. Box 35035 • Tulsa, Oklahoma 74153